THE VISION BOOK
Planner

GET CLEAR ON WHAT TRULY MATTERS AND
TAKE INSPIRED ACTION TO CREATE THE
LIFE YOUR HEART DESIRES

TAMMIE LEONARD
MINDSET MATTERS

WWW.INSPIREDACTION.CA

THE VISION BOOK PLANNER

Discounted bulk purchases are available. Contact Tammie at:

www.inspiredaction.ca

ISBN: 978-1-988675-38-1

STOKE Publishing

With gratitude for all the Beautiful Souls in my life,
you make my soul rich in countless ways.
You all deserve your Heart's Desires.

Before you get started...

I just want to say how grateful I am that you chose The Vision Book Planner. I truly believe we can all build a growth mindset through the clarity of our vision for a better life. Choosing The Vision Book Planner means you are choosing to create more love, happiness, positivity, success, wealth and gratitude in your life.

So here's to you and your successful vision journey. I wish you much love for yourself and success for your journey.

Cheers and remember,
Always Believe!
Tammie

CONTENTS

PART 1
My Great and Grateful Life

We make positive choices when we intertwine our environment with our vision.
- Tammie Leonard

Creating Your Vision Book means.....
Living and FEELING with Your Whole Heart.

Visioning isn't a time of simply daydreaming yourself into the life you hope to lead, it's a **clarity exercise** that brings a world of possibilities into your life. We attract what we think about all day long. You are not defined by your age, race, environment or your social status. **You are defined by your thoughts.** See it! Believe it! Create it! Achieve it! **Yes You Can!**

The Vision Book Planner is the keeper of your dreams, the safe place you can turn to again and again to remind you of what truly matters most to you. Never forget that **YOU MATTER** and so does the vision of your **heart's desires.**

Through the following pages and activities you will become clear on what matters most to you. This clarity will then be used to create the pages of your vision book and those pages will help you to **take inspired action** for the life you dream of, the life you were meant to live.

Your vision will become clear only when you can look into your own heart.....
Who looks outside dreams; who looks inside, awakes.
Carl Jung

The following pages will help you to **clear the noise, confusion and fear from your mind.** The exercises help you to become clear not on just what is safe, but what it is that your soul craves and your heart desires. Remember, you are attracting whatever is going on in your mind.

This Vision Book Planner is all about **INSPIRED ACTION.** Open your heart and mind to the unlimited possibilities waiting to unfold in your life. Now, grab your favorite beverage and perhaps a friend or two, get comfortable and **let's get started**! Your amazing life is waiting for you, it has always been there, simmering in the depths of your soul.

Life loves to be taken by the lapel and told, "I am with you kid, let's go."
Maya Angelou

Getting Clear On Your Vision
Grabbing Life by the Lapel

Knowing how you want to **FEEL** is a strong indication of clarity.

These feelings bring hope and inspiration to your dreams.

POSITIVE FEELINGS I WOULD WELCOME INTO MY LIFE.
For example, would you like to feel love, successful, peaceful, limitless, capable, healthy, abundance, daring, passion, glamorous, healed, safe, powerful, sexy, valuable, relaxed, devoted, adventurous, accepting, cherished, excited, unique, motivated or …..
Take a few minutes to really think about that and write those feelings below.

Positive feelings I would welcome into my life:

_____

_____

_____

_____

_____

So what is it you want? To **FEEL GOOD** of course.

Your successful VISION/GOAL/INTENTION is very important to your happiness so it must be one that makes you feel happy to the depths of your soul.

LET THERE BE SUNSHINE IN YOUR SOUL TODAY.

When you allow yourself to get very clear on what it is you want you automatically relax and feel a calmness come over you, body, mind and soul.
It is much easier to stick to the vision/goal/intention when you are creating that happy feeling from your head to your toes. **So let's see what it is that brings you joy.**

Complete each sentence.

*What I want most in life is

_____

_____

_____

*What I value most is

_____

_____

_____

*Other than time or money I would love more

_____

_____

_____

*Something that is different about me is

_____

_____

_____

*I really need to give myself permission to

_____

_____

_____

*The thing that I do most naturally is

_____

_____

_____

*Something that really makes me feel alive is

_____

_____

_____

*One way I get through the tough times is

_____

_____

_____

*My true happiness actually comes from

_____

_____

_____

Getting clear on what real happiness looks and feels like.

*Happiness looks like

_____

_____

_____

*Happiness feels like

_____

_____

_____

*Happiness smells like

_____

_____

_____

*The best feeling ever is

_____

_____

_____

*I feel true pride in myself when I

_____

_____

_____

*What really touches my heart and soul is

_____

_____

_____

*I know I am experiencing real happiness when I

_____

_____

_____

There are times when we are not feeling true happiness and that is okay because it is our wakeup call to regroup and do a self-check on our lives.

We must **get real** about what is interfering with our happiness so we can change it.

Brick Walls

*I feel most vulnerable when

_____

_____

_____

_____

*I am frightened of

_____

_____

_____

_____

*Something I keep locked away in my soul is

_____

_____

_____

_____

*I often feel I need to impress

_____

_____

_____

_____

*At times I feel lack of

_____

_____

_____

_____

*Something that causes me grief is

_____

_____

_____

_____

*A regular negative thought I have is

_____

_____

_____

_____

MINDSET MATTERS
FEEL GRATEFUL FOR THIS MOMENT-IT'S ALL YOU HAVE.

Getting specific on **WHAT** we are grateful for and **WHY** we are grateful for it increases our happy endorphins and helps us to get clear on what it is that brings us true joy.
So let's get clear. Take a few moments to really think about what you are grateful for and then jot down your thoughts in each of the four core areas of Daily Living (D.L.), Personal Wellness (P.W.), Soul Expression (S.E.) and Clan Connections (C.C.).

DAILY LIVING-possessions, travel, career, money, home, fashion

I am GRATEFUL for.....

_____

_____

_____

_____

I am GRATEFUL for these things because.....

_____

_____

_____

_____

In my DAILY LIVING I am not happy with these things.....

_____

_____

_____

_____

I know I am not happy because they make me feel.....

_____

_____

_____

PERSONAL WELLNESS-fitness, nutrition, mental health, soul, faith, time to self

I am GRATEFUL for.....

_____

_____

_____

_____

_____

I am GRATEFUL for these things because.....

_____

_____

_____

_____

_____

In my PERSONAL WELLNESS I am not happy with these things.....

_____

_____

_____

_____

_____

I know I am not happy because they make me feel.....

_____

_____

_____

_____

_____

SOUL EXPRESSION-hobbies, education, self-expression, soul art, spirituality

I am GRATEFUL for.....

_____

_____

_____

_____

_____

I am GRATEFUL for these things because.....

_____

_____

_____

_____

_____

In my SOUL EXPRESSION I am not happy with these things.....

_____

_____

_____

_____

_____

I know I am not happy because they make me feel.....

_____

_____

_____

_____

_____

CLAN CONNECTIONS-family, friends, community, work

I am GRATEFUL for…..

_____

_____

_____

_____

_____

I am GRATEFUL for these things because…..

_____

_____

_____

_____

_____

In my CLAN CONNECTIONS I am not happy with these things…..

_____

_____

_____

_____

_____

I know I am not happy because they make me feel…..

_____

_____

_____

_____

_____

Now describe how you would like to feel in each of the Four Core Areas.
Do you want to feel successful, peaceful, limitless, capable, healthy, abundance, daring, passion, glamorous, healed, safe, powerful, sexy, valuable, relaxed, devoted, adventurous, accepting, cherished, excited, unique, motivated.......... So many options. Jot down as many as come to mind in each of the following core areas.

DAILY LIVING-possessions, travel, career, money, home, fashion

_____

_____

_____

_____

_____

PERSONAL WELLNESS-fitness, nutrition, mental health, soul, faith, time to self

_____

_____

_____

_____

_____

SOUL EXPRESSION-hobbies, education, self-expression, soul art, spirituality

_____

_____

_____

_____

_____

CLAN CONNECTIONS-family, friends, community, work

_____

_____

_____

_____

_____

We may not have a say in the length of time we spend on Earth but we certainly do have a say in the depth and width of the love we share with the world.

So.....to be in your HAPPY PLACE, how would you have to feel in each of the Four Core Areas? To figure this out, choose three feelings from your previous activity for each of the following core areas of your life and write them below.

Daily Living

Personal Wellness

Soul Expression

Clan Connections

Four CORE HAPPY FEELINGS I would need to feel to experience true happiness in my life:
(Choose one feeling from each core area of the above activity to create your four CORE HAPPY FEELINGS.)

Daily Living (D.L.)	Personal Wellness (P.W.)	Soul Expression (S.E.)	Clan Connections (C.C.)

Complete the following sentences using the above CORE HAPPY FEELINGS choices.

*To feel _____, _____, _____ &_____
          D.L.   P.W.   S.E.   C.C.

in my **Daily Living** I would need to be, do or have

_____

_____

_____

*To feel _____, _____, _____ &_____
                    D.L.   P.W.   S.E.   C.C.

in my **Personal Wellness** I would need to be, do or have

_____

_____

_____

*To feel _____, _____, _____ &_____
                    D.L.   P.W.   S.E.   C.C.

in my **Soul Expression** I would need to be, do or have

_____

_____

_____

*To feel _____, _____, _____ &_____
                    D.L.   P.W.   S.E.   C.C.

in my **Clan Connections** I would need to be, do or have

_____

_____

_____

Now you will check in on what it is that stands in the way of your heart's desires.

What has stopped you from feeling _____, _____, _____
                                                         D.L.   **P.W.**   **S.E.**
and _____ in your daily living? Include...past experiences, past relationships, past
          C.C.
failures and past brick walls.

Daily Living: possessions, travel, career, money, home, fashion

_____

_____

_____

_____

_____

Personal Wellness: fitness, nutrition, mental health, soul, faith, time to self

_____

_____

_____

_____

_____

Soul Expression: hobbies, education, self-expression, soul art, spirituality

_____

_____

_____

_____

_____

Clan Connections: family, friends, community, work

_____

_____

_____

_____

_____

I WILL MAKE THE LIFE IN MY YEARS COUNT.

In the following areas of your life, what successes have you had that made you feel

_____, _____, _____ and _____?
   D.L.   P.W.   S.E.   C.C.

Daily Living: possessions, travel, career, money, home, fashion

_____

_____

_____

_____

Personal Wellness: fitness, nutrition, mental health, soul, faith, time to self

_____

_____

_____

_____

Soul Expression: hobbies, education, self-expression, soul art, spirituality

_____

_____

_____

_____

Clan Connections: family, friends, community, work

_____

_____

_____

_____

****

Being **GRATEFUL** helps you create those happy vibes needed to create your positive growth mindset in order to achieve your goals and live your vision.

In each core area choose a goal you would like to achieve over the next month or year and add to it which Core Happy Feeling it will bring with it and WHY you would be grateful to achieve that goal. Your why is very important to your success.
OPTION: you may choose to complete or tweak this next section after you have finished creating your vision book planner in the section ahead.

Daily Living Goal-

_____

I will feel _____ and **grateful** when I have achieved this

goal because _____

Personal Wellness Goal-

_____

I will feel _____ and **grateful** when I have achieved this

goal because _____

Soul Expression Goal-

_____

I will feel _____ and **grateful** when I have achieved this

goal because _____

Clan Connection Goal-

_____

I will feel _____ and **grateful** when I have achieved this

goal because _____

****

Connect With Your Inner Thought Power and Open Your Heart To Your Endless Possibilities.

Using your four **CORE HAPPY FEELINGS** complete the following **AFFIRMATION.**

Today I choose to feel _____, _____,
  D.L. P.W.

_____ **and** _____ **because**
  S.E. C.C.

I AM WORTH IT!

Connecting to Your Inner Thought Power

Before moving on to creating your vision and connecting to your Inner Thought Power it is a must that you take some focused quiet time to go back and review your previous clarity exercises. Take time to release those negative thoughts and brick walls as they serve no purpose, you have acknowledged them and now it is time to let them go. Move forward to soak in the warmth of your Successes and Core Happy Feelings. Let your soul play with the visions/goals/intentions of your heart's desires so you can take Inspired Action to move forward to create the new HAPPY YOU in the following Vision Book Planner section.

Cheers to you and your Heart's Desires! You've got this!

PART 2: Creating Your Vision Book
Option A and B

Put your heart, mind and soul into even the smallest acts.
This is the secret of success.
Swami Sivananda

The Vision Book Planner is so much more than scattered pictures. It can be words, phrases, drawings, stickers, quotes, photos, power words, computer images, core value words, glitter and whatever it is your **creative soul** would like to include. There is no right or wrong way to make a vision book so **let's get started!**

Steps to Creating Your Vision Book.

OPTION A.....Yes, life is full options.

1. Start by collecting the necessary materials you will need such as a variety of magazines, paper for drawings, photos, colored pens or markers, stickers, glitter, a good quality glue stick and scissors.

2. Get comfortable and eliminate any possible distractions. Put on some of your favorite music and review your findings from the previous clarity exercises as this will get you in the mindset needed to fire you up when creating your soul's vision of your heart's desires.

3. Surround yourself with a variety of magazines. Now without rushing simply flip through those magazines and rip out any and all words or images that catch your eye. Simply rip them out and pile them up. When you feel that you have collected as many as you would like for now go through the pile and trim the words, phrases or pictures you found. After this you can sort them into the areas of **HOME, CLAN CONNECTIONS, HEALTH, TRAVEL & ADVENTURE, SPIRIT & SOUL EXPRESSION, CAREER & EDUCATION, and YOUR HEART'S DESIRES.**

4. You will then arrange and rearrange and glue your pictures, phrases, words, drawings, photos on the following appropriate pages. Remember, there are no rules to how this is done. You may embellish your pages any way you like. Let your creative side soar.

OPTION B.....Create your very own personalized vision scrapbook.
You may choose to use the following pages for some written brainstorming space and then use a simple scrapbook to cut, paste, color, draw, sparkle, embellish and **CREATE YOUR VERY OWN PERSONALIZED VISION BOOK.** The vision book is about letting your soul breathe and find its way. This is a process that should be enjoyed. So let your soul be bold, be creative, be brave, whether that be on the pages of this book or your very own personalized vision scrap book. Remember, **life is about choices and options.** Choose to be daring and watch the magic fall into place creating your **Heart's Desires.**

Cheers to you and the magic of your soul. Let your dance with the universe begin!

HOME
POSSESSIONS, SPACE, LOCATION
(Glue the pieces of your vision here.)

Each morning we are born again,
What we do today matters most.
Buddha

CLAN CONNECTIONS

FAMILY, FRIENDS, COMMUNITY, WORK

(Glue the pieces of your vision here.)

Your success and happiness starts with you.
Helen Keller

HEALTH – NUTRITION & FITNESS

MENTAL HEALTH, PHYSICAL HEALTH

(Glue the pieces of your vision here.)

Our food should be our medicine and our medicine should be our food.
Hippocrates

TRAVEL & ADVENTURE
VACATIONS, MONEY, TIME, RESTAURANTS, DESTINATIONS
(Glue the pieces of your vision here.)

As our days unfold, so do the years of our lives.
Tammie Leonard

SPIRIT & SOUL EXPRESSION

FAITH, HOBBIES, ART, SPIRITUALITY, SELF-EXPRESSION, PEACE

(Glue the pieces of your vision here.)

It is not the stars that hold our destiny but in ourselves.
William Shakespeare

CAREER & EDUCATION
MONEY, TIME, LOCATION, EXPERTISE
(Glue the pieces of your vision here.)

You are today where your thoughts brought you;
You will be tomorrow where your thoughts take you.
James Allen

HEART'S DESIRES

SLEEP, FASHION, BOOKS, ART, POSSESSIONS, anything your HEART DESIRES

(Glue the pieces of your vision here.)

This above all-to thine own self be true.
William Shakespeare

Part 3: Creating Gratitude in Your Life
Yes You Can

To be thankful, expressing thankfulness, to celebrate the present moment.

Gratitude
**can transform common days into thanksgiving,
turn routine jobs into joy, and
change ordinary opportunities into**
Blessings.
William Arthur Ward

Using the same instructions given for creating your vision book pages, grab some magazines and then cut and paste, draw or write, all the things in your life you are **GRATEFUL FOR** onto the following pages. Or, choose **OPTION B** and add gratitude to your very own **personalized vision scrapbook.**

GRATITUDE

Piglet noticed that even though he had a very small heart, it could hold a rather large amount of gratitude.
A.A. Milne

GRATITUDE

Feeling gratitude and not expressing it is like wrapping a present and not giving it.
William Arthur Ward

GRATITUDE

We can only be said to be alive in those moments when our hearts are conscious of our treasures.
Thornton Wilder

Part 4: Thoughts for Today
Journaling Your Heart's Desires
Use the following pages to share your thoughts and heart's desires.

If you want to know where your heart is,
Look to where your mind goes when it wanders.
Unknown

_____

_____

_____

_____

_____

_____

_____

_____

_____

_____

_____

_____

_____

_____

_____

_____

_____

_____

_____

_____

_____

_____

_____

_____

_____

_____

_____

_____

_____

_____

I can shake off everything as I write.
My sorrows disappear, my courage is reborn.
Anne Frank

_____

_____

_____

_____

_____

_____

_____

_____

_____

_____

_____

_____

_____

_____

_____

_____

_____

_____

_____

_____

_____

_____

_____

Fill your paper with the breathings of your heart.
William Wordsworth

We become what we think about all day long.
Ralph Waldo Emerson

Today you are you! That is truer than true!
There is no one alive that is you-er than you!
Dr. Seuss

Wherever you go, go with all your heart.
Confucius

_____

_____

_____

_____

_____

_____

_____

_____

_____

_____

_____

_____

_____

_____

_____

_____

_____

_____

_____

_____

_____

_____

_____

Your thoughts on paper give the universe something to play with.
Tammie Leonard

_____
_____
_____
_____
_____
_____
_____
_____
_____
_____
_____
_____
_____
_____
_____
_____
_____
_____
_____
_____
_____
_____
_____
_____
_____
_____

Thought is action in rehearsal.
Sigmund Freud

When I let go of what I am, I become what I might be.
Lao Tzu

Let your written words whisper the desires of your heart.
Tammie Leonard

Part 5: Now What?
It's not over yet!

Now you get to sit back and look at the beautiful and inspiring life about to unfold before you. Are you done now? Nope! You are never finished with your vision book. Not only can you continue to repeat this activity at any time but it is a must that you continually review and envision (daily, monthly, and yearly) all that you have learned from your clarity exercises and the visuals on your vision book pages. And then, of course, you will take steps of **INSPIRED ACTION** so that your life will be filled with your **CORE HAPPY FEELINGS** of.....

(D.L.)_____, (P.W.)_____,

(S.E.)_____ & (C.C.)_____.

Now, just in case you need a little extra help with this amazing vision of yours, I have included a little **TO DO LIST** to help you follow through with the success of your vision for a **HAPPY INSPIRED LIFE.**

MINDSET MATTERS and so does your TO DO LIST!

Time passes. What are you doing daily with your time to feel _____,

                                                    (D.L.)

_____, _____ and _____?

        (P.W.)   (S.E.)   (C.C.)

1. Fill in your calendar with those little things that need to be done to reach your goal. This will help to keep you focused and accountable to your goal. Put your vision/goals/intentions into your calendar.

    Little changes make big changes possible.

2. Create a mantra that you can repeat to yourself when the going gets tough.

    "I am stronger than this!"

3. Write affirmations on flash cards and go through them each morning and evening to remind you why it is that you are sticking to the vision/goals/intentions. Your WHY will keep you going when you just want to give up.

    "I am eating a healthy breakfast because I want to feel strong and energetic."

4. Find a soul sister that keeps you accountable.

    Friends will lift you up when you've forgotten how to fly.

5. Use sticky notes with the feelings on them that you want to feel and put them everywhere.

    Brave! Energized! Confident! Peaceful! Strong!

6. Mirror work. Write those happy feelings and affirmations on your mirror. Let them be the first thing you see in the morning and the last thing you see at night.

I choose to be hopeful and optimistic!

7. Keep a gratitude journal. Remember gratitude tells our bodies to create those happy endorphins and those happy feelings keep us charging towards our visions.
When you wake up in the morning think of three things you are grateful for in the day ahead (Yes plan ahead to have a good day.) and when you go to sleep at night think of three things you are grateful for that happened that day as it will help you to fall asleep peacefully.

A grateful heart is a happy heart.

8. Schedule journal time. Put those thoughts and worries that seem to be taking up space in that beautiful mind into a journal and then close it up. They will be safe there, no longer able to bother you. Or, write about your plans for the future and all the amazing events about to happen in your life.

I want to write, but more than that, I want to bring out all kinds of things that lie buried deep in my heart.   Anne Frank

9. Clean up your messes and incompletes, they are distractions to your success. That might mean cleaning out drawers, finishing those little projects like paint touch-ups, organizing your closet or perhaps completing your homework. Clean up your distractions and you make room for your vision/goals/intentions.

a.k.a..... To Do List

10. Reward yourself for even your small successes. Great achievements come about because of small wins, so buy yourself your favorite magazine or a specialty coffee.

You deserve it!

LIFE ISN'T ABOUT FINDING YOURSELF.
LIFE IS ABOUT CREATING YOURSELF.
George Bernard Shaw

Part 6: My Wish For You

When you get into a tight place and everything goes against you,
Till it seems as though you couldn't hang on a minute longer,
Don't give up then,
For that is just the place and time the tide will turn.
Harriet Beecher Stowe

Every day is a chance to grow and move forward with a positive growth mindset. My wish for you is that after walking through the steps of the Vision Book Planner you will have created a vision that gives you that, 'I AM SO HAPPY' feeling because that is what we all deserve. We all deserve to wake up every morning with that feeling of, 'I AM SO HAPPY TO BE ALIVE.' This is it, there is no dress rehearsal. What are you waiting for? There is no time like today, after all, that is all we have is today. So stop waiting for the perfect moment in time. This is it, this is your time!

So cheers to you and your HAPPY LIFE!
Remember, you deserve your Heart's Desires.

Tammie

YOU CAN FIND MORE INSPIRATION when you visit my website at:

www.inspiredaction.ca to learn about my books and services as well as my blog and additional inspirational resources.

Books available for you to create inspired action also by Tammie Leonard:
- Thoughts to Give you Wings-The Time to be Happy is Now, The Place to be Happy is Here
- 365 Days For Me-Yes You Can
- A Year of Gratitude-Choose To Be Happy
- Choices-A Yearly Student Success Planner

Sign up for my free challenge called **How to Change Your Mindset** at www.inspiredaction.ca .

Connect on Social Media
Facebook.com/inspired action motivation and consulting
Instagram @tammie_leonard

About the Author

Tammie Leonard is a retired teacher, motivational speaker, inspired action coach, author, Certified Canfield Success Principles Trainer and Coach and the founder of Inspired Action Motivation and Consulting.

Overcoming past struggles with anxiety, agoraphobia, cancer, goal setting and other crazy life events, led Tammie to write her first book, *Thoughts to Give You Wings*. Tammie's passion for helping others believe, have faith in themselves and create clarity for their goals led her to write three other motivational books; *365 Days For Me*, *A Year of Gratitude and Choices-A Student Success Planner*.

Tammie lives in Prince Albert, Saskatchewan and when she is not writing or coaching people to create clarity in their lives, Tammie loves spending time with her two adult children, Landon and Lexi, her husband Tim and her chocolate lab Lily.

Find out more about Tammie and her passion for changing one mindset at a time at, www.inspiredaction.ca